Another Lid to a Potless Existence

Collected Poetry 2006 – 2012

also featuring:

The List

T.R. Dailey

Published by Ætherbound Books

www.TRDailey.com

Copyright © 2014 T.R. Dailey

All rights reserved.

ISBN: 0615963080
ISBN-13: 978-0615963082

To my mother and father,

My existence depended on them.

ACKNOWLEDGMENTS

First off, I must thank my mother for our amazing ghost and alien conversations and for always laughing while playing words like "Clitorus" on family game night.

I thank my fiancé, Jose L. Marin, who continues to love me although I make weird noises and bound around the house flailing my arms late at night while caffeinated. And I continue to love him because he always joins me.

I must thank Brooke James for her unstoppable charm and abundant strength through dark nights and Chad Brown for his philosophical wit and poetically rebellious existence. They have made many a contribution to this book and both hold very special places in my heart.

A huge thanks to Tom Bowyer for taking me on the winter camping trip that ignited my words and melted my boots and for saving my life when that car barreled toward us going the wrong way on the freeway.

Thank you to Glynnis Campbell for not calling the police when we had to break into our own house next door after locking ourselves out during a dog-walk, but also for a gentle push toward an open door I had not seen.

And thank you to Peter Voerman for allowing me to showcase his stunning cliff-jumping photo in this book.

Additional thanks to San Diego State University, the Starbucks on College Ave., and all my friends that attended the epic Halloween at Leah's in 2006.

CONTENTS

POEMS

The Way It Should Be

Look at me, a quick glance, make it brief.

I don't smoke pot.
I don't get drunk.
I don't have sex.
I don't have a boyfriend.
I've never been with a girl.
I don't daydream
or sleep
or itch
or get sick
and vomit in a box in my closet.
I don't bite my nails.
I've never stuffed household objects inside me
or snorted goldfish crackers like cocaine during church.
I'm never hurt or cold or fearful
or any other emotion.
I have no memories.
I have no imperfections.
I don't have a scar under my right breast.
My back isn't riddled with acne scars.
I don't worry about my vision
or the circumference of my torso
or my tiny hands and plump toes.
I don't bother noticing how big my arms are
or the rolls on my back
or how pale I look when I get out of the shower.
As a matter of fact, I don't even take showers.
I'm never naked.
I don't shit or piss or menstruate.
I don't have friends
or parents
or grandparents.

Instead, all you see is me.

Blonde hair in the breeze
Green eyes framed in black glasses
A clear pretty face
With full lips that compliment a pearly white grin.
Me, dressed in a shirt
Corduroys and chucks.

A brief glance,
Just me, that's all you see.

And maybe it's better that way.
And maybe that's all you should see.
And maybe that's the way I want it
And maybe that's the way it should be.

The Glass Door

He looked so foolish
Bright red
When he stepped back
From his mistake.

A drunken stupor
Silly goose
And we couldn't stop
Our laughing.

$1.00 Pumpkin

Little Moon Pie
Orange and sweet
A smile on his rump
Will sit upon my desk this year
And share my Halloween.

Heliocentric Hallucinations Orbiting the Loo

My body is detached
from my head.
The shower curtain is
Orange.
I hear noises that
aren't
really there.
There are people talking.
British accents
in a fury
about my ears.
An alligator's
teeth
chomping
telling me not to
write.
Is it possible?
He tastes like
chocolate and
oatmeal – the breath
of a bear.
Licking the cross.
The stairs are dangerous
to newcomers.
I'm so comfortable on the floor.
The kids are upstairs
fucking like wild animals.
It's like a steel cage
my stomach.
One after another
like maple syrup
coating the train station.

I'm flying
out of the sack
of plastered flesh,
Toward the sky
the blue
the ocean
the two sapphire gems
you invite me to.
And I can see the air
flowing into our lungs
pink like cotton sugar.
The oxygen runs through
veins,
through life –
yours.
And flows out again –
mine
like stainless steel
lightning ribbons
that we can cheat
chest to chest
with only stars
as witness.
Shock.
Something is watching
and you're not really here
in this room…
Were you ever?
The walls of beans
disturb me
papered and peeling
boiled through lifetimes of
showers.
BING!

The computer is now
on and alit.

I trust in that clock
which is telling
nay, yelling
the fact that it is
the beginning of
tomorrow.

Pay Attention

The world is calling your soul.

Butterflies and Dragonflies
Toads and Tiger Lilies
Treasures hidden
All Around
Of every shape and size

Corner Cobwebs, Flower Fields
A tale that should be told
Far from hatred
Far from home
A little dream of gold

Listen, smile, speak, and laugh
Learn a world away
Look around you
Pace yourself
The world moves quick today

Only the Details make Us Different

We both have furry slippers
Hers are red
And mine are black

To Paul Bunyan, "I smite thee", Love God.

A lumberjack
A naughty nurse
Pirates and white rabbits
Will gather once a year
And commence in silly habits.

A shining knight
A Scottish kilt
Hugh Hefner and a pimp
All stand around with beer
Eating cocktail sauce and shrimp

Half a Jekyll
Half a Hyde
A cat that's not a human
Hockey Player, Zombie Guy
And Potter's wand is lumen

Bony Batman
Drunken Hulk
Combative Bumblebees
Two black angels dancing 'round
A white one in her skivvies

Insane asylum escapee
Cleopatra and her husband
Will all bear witness to this test
When God threw a cinder block upon him…

Concern

My boots are smudged
My wings are broken
But I will continue trudging
Through the darkness.

And you will look
Out your window in twilight
And see a Dark Angel
Skipping in the street.

The Trip

Gonna catch a high
in a bed in the back room.

Gonna catch a ride
to the sky.

Gonna jump the cliffs
on a live-wire pole.

Gonna sail
to the brilliant end.

12 Minutes at Starbucks

12 fancy pine trees
11 people sitting
10 coffee blends
9 city buses
8 giant tote bags
7 heels in rain
6 cell phones ringing
5 in a meeting
4 paramedics
3 hard workers
2 Cups of coffee
And a poodle with a wheelchair…

Not a Hippie

Back in the day,
Hippies wore their shirts
Long and free.
But nowadays
Thanks to society
And his obsession
With sexuality
This girl knotted
A tie-dyed gimmick
With a rubber band
So her curves were there
For her class to see.

A happy face.

And you thought that maybe
You could live with it.
A simplistic problem,
Nothing to worry over…

Nobody would care,
They're so happy,
Don't bring them down
To your level.

You didn't want to be selfish,
But look where it got you.
Someone would have cared,
Someone.

It will go away in a while.
You've dealt with it before.
You know the routine
That will keep you sane.

And now you're stranded.
There's no turning back
And no one can care
Anymore.

Just be strong.
Life will float by.
This will end just like
Everything else.

A better place.

There's still more
Leave now
And progress.

The Last Drop

I went to take a swig
Of my Hot Chocolate
But there was only
A drop left
And it was cold
And powdery.
So I no longer have
Creamy Hot Chocolate
Instead I have
Chunky Cold Cocoa.

Sit-Ups

Make me twitch
Like I've just orgasmed
All over my gym pants
I sweat and breathe hard
While my heart pounds
And everyone can watch
As I lie back in my exhaustion.

Fluttered Papers

Hold them together
A notebook
Spiral bound
Fire engine red

A paperclip
A staple
A metal clasp

Something must hold them together
Like the sun holds together
The warm sand at my feet

A Book's Binding

Pinching the nerve endings
Of your soul
Spilled onto the pages:
Divergent whispers
Tired dreams
Hushed stories
A triumphant world to hold.

Anticipating

So much wants to come through
At once.
I want to shout
Raise my hands and shout
Like a musical
Quality.
Like being so excited that you can’t
Express yourself.

SCREAM!

And then dance
Because nothing else is working.
Focus ebbs
My chest wells up like the floats
On the Macy’s Day Parade.

Something New Entirely

My whole world stopped,
Do you even know what you're saying?
Can you hear yourself?
A shockwave
A pause in my heartbeat
My world slowed to a stop
Hers too,
Together we watched
You just kept talking
No stopping
So shocking
We waited
We watched
My world slowly resurfaced
The sounds returned
People began moving
And you
Aren't aware
As we glance at each other
Our eyes wide, astonished
That you stopped the world.

Chapped Lips

The torture of a cold day
Deserves nothing more
Than the tender warmth of night
A night that I carry
Upon my lips
Lips that sit patiently
Upon my face
While I wait for you
And you're embrace.

1942

A waltz, a walk
A room with a lock
Silenced as a group
Together, alone

The heat, the hell
The gaseous smell
Choked as a group
Together, alone

A fire, a flame
A cheapened name
Burned as a group
Together, alone

Another Lid to a Potless Existence

earth earth earth earth earth earth earth
earth earth earth earth earth earth ea
earth earth earth earth earth ear e
earth earth earth earth earth ea
earth earth earth earth eart
earth earth earth earth e
earth earth earth eart
earth earth earth
earth earth ea
earth earth
earth e
eart
e

air air air air air air air air air air air air
air air air air air air air air air air air
air air air air air air air air air air
air air air air air air air air air
air air air air air air air air
air air air air air air air
air air air air air air
air air air air air
air air air air
air air air
i air
ir
r

Revolving

Watermelon Life

Overtly disastrous world

Breathing together, complex heartbeat

Trustworthy elephants, death without beauty

Mother Nature sighs; tumor develops: malignant

Fools. Oscillating lifestyle, blindness settled – ignorant bliss

Knowledge counts scapegoated blessings upon toilet paper victories

An endangered love, shockwave from existence – evolutionary time catch

Mom’s formula: revitalizing zest, essence of soul, affection

Attention to quintessence, ideal focus: cherry pickers

Honey-sweetened breath rises, celebrated patience

Transcendentalism at its finest hour

One Expensive Orange Popsicle

Difficult Harlequin Dream

Not Improbable

Attachment

w
wat
water
water wat
water water
water water wat
water water water
water water water wat
water water water water
water water water water wa
water water water water water
water water water water water wa
water water water water water water

fi
fire
fire fire
fire fire fire
re fire fire fire
e fire fire fire fire
fire fire fire fire fire
fire fire fire fire fire fire
fire fire fire fire fire fire fire
fire fire fire fire fire fire fire fire
fire fire fire fire fire fire fire fire fire
fire fire fire fire fire fire fire fire fire fire
e fire fire fire fire fire fire fire fire fire fire

Vengeance

Oh it's like sugar
How it rolls off my lips
The sweetness serenades my soul
A device against bitter black words
Like coffee on a hot day.

Yearning

The city lights
Are so bright
In the night
It's always a fight
To be more powerful than
The stars in the sky
That we yearn to fly
But we cannot escape
The confines
Of the concrete jungle
That we call our lives.

Unknown

The fire inside is ever flowing
Because we can't figure out
Where we're ever going
And the clouds in the sky
Are always all knowing
As they watch us
Stumble, trip, and fall
And they hold their laughter
Behind their wall
That we can't quite touch
Yet we reach for such
And we fight for the life
That we yearn to have
And one day we hope to find
A ladder.

Direct Emotional Intervention

"pain"
The only way to look at
the toy box.

About Writing

It's a memory
that hasn't been made yet,
but you already know
all the details to it.
A book that holds
my imagination
my dreams
my hopes
my goals
my heart
my soul
my life
and in order to write it
set it all aside
and enjoy.
Difficulties abound
but it will come
like a fleeting gesture
of the wrist
amid quick conversation
before it's lost
to otherworldly tribulations

Long Way Home

Salute
Say fuck the world
I'm outta here

Where does the freeway end
If you take it all the way?
Where can I go to leave
When I decide to stay?

Can I drop my world
My soul my life
To step off the wagon
Fight for paradise

Salute
Say fuck the world
I'm outta here

Over mountains over seas
Over troubles over pleas
Over sickness over strife
Over drama over life

Where could I go
When money's thin?
Revolution afoot
And begin again

Salute
Say fuck the world
I'm outta here

THE PHOTOGRAPH

The following three poems are written while viewing and describing a photograph. The photograph, at the time, contained unknown people, an unknown photographer, and an unknown location. It was also unbeknownst at the time that this photo was only a partial.

The following three poems were written in succession about this photograph.

Water's Edge

Flight into the vast unknown

Anticipation
Exhilaration
Illumination
Ostentation
Undulation

Vowels afoot
We're young at heart.

Leather plumes, leather plumes
Outlandish attire
But the crags bite and scorn
like magma fire

A dare, a fare, a silly scare

A step toward the edge,
A leap of faith

Suspended motion
Trapped in time
Stop this wily nursery rhyme!
Turn back
Turn around
I say I'm a sheep
I want out
I want out
My heart rises, my leap

I fly through the air
Bare back warm in the sun
A breeze up my shorts
My adventure soon to be done

The Photograph

I once had a professor
who hated ambiguous poetry
“Concrete details!”
“Show don’t tell!”
My poetry was never successful
with him.
Then one day he told me
to describe a scene…
Three thin boys flying through the air
bare backs, gray swim shorts,
and leather shoes strapped to their feet
like Achilles.
They must have had a running start
to get high off the cliff –
A cliff covered with barnacles
and small sharp rocks imbedded
on the surface.
The dark ripples
stretched out in front of them
like the ocean.
Only this ocean is so clear,
looking down you can see
the rocks shimmering
in the sunlight.
The boys
with their arms outstretched
risk the drop.
Their bones completely visible
caught in time.
The bumps of their spines
The sharp angles of shoulder blades
reveal their hungry thirst
for the adventure that lay below them.

But I told my professor
that it was no good
I can't describe such
a scene.

Off Colored Soulless Dimension

(written with Brooke James and Chad Brown)

Once there was a boy named Sue
One Two Three Jumped
As they leapt to their death
They had no idea what they left behind
Why are they wearing shoes?
Mother realized it was too late for an abortion
Of their mission
They leapt to escape
The oncoming traffic
Of the mind

These malnourished children
Saw a fish in the water
They wanted
They will surely be lovers one day
Little is known about the third
Except that one day he would grow up to be
Thomas A. Edison
But he died off the cliff
And that's why there will never be light
And this was typed by candlelight

Copyright
Peter Voerman

CAMPING

Camping in Winter

You can't see anything
But fire.
The heat so close
Yet the cold: indescribable.
Hands like blocks of wood –
Cold and immobile.
Numb,
We feel nothing.
The sensation of urination
Persists in my lower abdomen
"I can't hang" – he said
At the next campsite.
I wish our bed had more air.
Air.
It feels so good.
Cold.
Smells of
Firewood,
Barbecue,
And horse shit.
The boys are so loud
At the fire
And I can hear him
Calling my name
In the dark,
"Almost 7:00"

Night Unreal

I Float
when I close my eyes
on a ship far out
on the Ptolemaic River
and the stars
are fluorescent…
And the night is a million
jelly beans
glued together.
Licorice.

A loner

In the midst…
I must acclimate
To the solitude
I will respect
It's love forever.
Like a black
Toboggan sled.

How can I describe the trees
That grow in crisp air?
The yellow leaves
Dance in winter wind.
They're tall and mighty
And content.

A great night

The crispy cool
Of firecrackers
And the dancing musical
voices.
Beautiful.
Reverberance.
Amazement.

Frozen

It was so strange
waking up in an icebox
this Antarctic morning.
I could see my breath
floating listlessly from my lungs
and dancing
into the winter sun.
My goosebumps
have goosebumps
which cast shadows
on my numb limbs.
I can't feel the 20
degree air anymore.
And so I remain
jacketless.
The moment I notice
is when I realize
there is more warmth
than what I'm feeling
and I curl up under
the down blankets
like an ice cube
waiting to melt.

Intoxicated

If I let my eyes close
The steam rises from
My mouth
And everyone tells me
That I'm drunk
And need water
But I no longer
Believe them.
If I refuse
To close my eyes
Then the earth is warm
And life is good.

A New Night Calls

No one is there to pick up
Instead the phone rings
Into the quiet
Stars,
Mountains,
Nature
Tend to take over
You allow it.

And as the lights fade
And the houses awaken
To a nonexistent crowing
The phone stops ringing
And the stars retreat to slumber –
I retreat
Wondering
If anything
Was fulfilled
And
If anything
Ever is.

MORE POETRY

Courage

She looked out over the ocean sparkling.
She rose to her feet and turned to face the world.
There was nowhere to go now,
But through the hurricane of dreams.

Stars

Mere bits of glitter,
fall to the ground in heaps
of forgotten dreams –
Dreams yearning to be picked up
and shared with the world

There's a blimp crashing outside
My window
Into the clouds.

Illiterate

Writing by moonlight
Seems difficult
If there is a roof over your head.
It was only last night
That I knew
Lights shimmered from my mind
In glittery ribbons
And lifted my hair
From my shoulders
Weightless and feathery.

Reading in sunshine
Seems difficult
If there is a roof over your head.
Yet it was today
That I realized
If you close your eyes,
Read with your soul
Feel the words kiss your ears,
You may feel
The breath of the writer on your neck.

Awaiting Normal

Once the eerie silence of the streets
completes its reverberation,
I think my life,
the conceptual indifference
I hide
behind my corneas,
will begin to settle back down
to normalcy.

Oh what brilliance!
What juvenile bliss!
A hummingbird
Whispering in the mist.

Nostalgic Forest

Can we walk the original footpath?
Can't we just go back?
Return to that spot,
And walk it again?
Our footsteps, surely,
Have washed away in all this
Rain
And heat
And pain
And grown over with
Moss
Mushrooms
Centipede poop.
Can't we just go back
And walk it again?
Turn off into a different
Bush
or tree
or broken log
or boulder
And just try again?
Would we make the wrong
Footholds
All over again?
Was the footpath we chose
Truly the only option
At the time
Or could we have hacked
Away
And ended up some place
Better?
Would we have found that
Mystical waterfall?

Will we ever?

A dramatic change in
Pace.
A dramatic change in
Handwriting.
Makes you wonder –
If the heartbeat
Is true.

How many people in the world are alone right now?

I Saw That

The pick of
That nose
That wedgy
That unpopular music
That individuality

You hide it.
Don't watch.
No one saw.
You can keep it to yourself.

But me,
I saw that.

Drum Circle

Free from the rhythms
The drum still beats
The fire still dances
Hearts pound as one
Intensity explodes, variation
Power rises, vivid life
Feet fall, vivid death
Wild dances
Chanting souls
Free from the rhythms
The drum still beats.

Subjective Importance

The rocks and ground
that hold me above
that six foot drop
are blue and cold.
The remnants of
shining star light
trickles slowly
through the atmosphere
hoping to make the night
more enjoyable.
The mountains like
Hollywood backdrops
of some unfamous movie
hope to be millionaires
someday.

It's so weird when my lines
Squish at the end of a page.
It makes my thoughts feel
Squishy too.

So Sure

Of something
That never
Is
Was
Will be
And yet
So sure.
The chances
Of happenstance
Are slim
If you only
Chance it
Once.

He speaks
To my heart
Direct
Metaphors,
But ignores
Mine.

The Hole

I feel like digging myself into a hole.
Nay,
I'm already in one.
Curled up
And stuffed in
An uncomfortable world
With an insurmountable
Affinity to small cats.

What am I doing?

I don't know how to write
this poetry…
yet I am…
free verse, free form, realist crap
that's rolling toward the gutter
where a hundred dollar bill lay crumpled
stuck to the shit-stained jargon
that critics value over the bill itself.
I continue
Door's closed
Get out!
My nakedness
offends.
Go ahead,
sleep with them,
like lovers on the alps
as music ignites
the dancing
of my pink caterpillar fingers
shaking their blue lunula tails
that produce this silken text.

Day to Day

Mundane.
Change is
inevitable
and yet
nonexistent;
only in one's
Mind

Physically Impossible

A hatch of fire
Ridiculous.
Time engulfed
Ridiculous.
A situation enthroned
Ridiculous.
A happy end
Ridiculous.
Ridiculous.
Ridiculous.

Finder's fee, He said

10 percent,
He said.
Los Angeles
Sure things
Easy Money
He said.
Fuck that
I said.
Staying put.
Friends, food, love
I said.
And a 1 year house lease.

Last Drink

Although blacklighted
A patron sighs.
Only when the cold metal floor
Is introduced
Does the patron cry.
Injustice.
Outrage.
Such a sour taste in my mouth.
And somewhere
An asshole dies.

Idling

And so you sit waiting
for something to happen.
Some miracle.
Some piece
of inspiration.
You have to wonder if you've lost it.
Oodles
Bags
Weighty golden bundles
Of talent.
You were so sure,
So convinced
That you had talent
Dripping out of your
Rolled up sleeves.
Gobs
Stacks
overflowing gem-encrusted ladles full
Of talent.
Was it all gone?
Used up, washed away
Mixed up in Sunday's
White load
and tossed out
like dryer lint.
Could it be as you sit there
Contemplating
Mysteries
During a hot muggy summer evening
Listening to
Cicadas
Crickets
Frogs

Whatever.
Is it possible all of your
Dripping goblets of dew covered blissful talent
Ebbed away?
A quiet departure.

It's Not a Hello

So here in lies the rest of it
The ends, farewells, goodbyes
The see you laters, take care for nows,
Toodles, cheers and sighs.
Adios, Au revoir, Tot Ziens, Adeus
Arrivederci il mio amico
Auf Wiedersehens too.
So this is it, until next time
I love you, I truly do.

featuring:

THE LIST

The List is a series of quotes and phrases, which keep us sane in a world of chaos.

The List is joy.

CREATED BY:

BROOKE JAMES (DARK GREY)
AND
T.R. DAILEY (LIGHT GREY)

Written over a span of a year in colorful permanent marker on lined paper and taped haphazardly to the walls of a dorm hallway, The List was created as something to help us push through the hard times. We searched out beauty and strength, wrote it down, and, when we needed it most, used it to remind ourselves to be grateful and to appreciate what is hidden by clouded eyes and minds.

The World is Calling Your Soul

Pay attention to the butterflies

Sleep is beautiful!

"It's like rain upon the moon"

A conversation I had:

- "Would you rather be ordinary or perfect?"
- "Neither. I'd rather be me."

Live in the moment

Unhappiness is a threatening lifestyle, move on successfully

Appreciate the little things, you never really know what you have until it's gone.

"Sprite understands me"

– Comm video

PAGE 2 OF THE LIST WAS STOLEN, IT SAID:

(Brooke in Italic. T.R. in Bold)

15 million people starve to death per year and my stomach hurts because I'm full.

I like to walk barefoot through the grass when no one's looking

Stay spontaneous

Everyone can see the beauty in the world.

Everyone has a soul

when they're alone.

But people need to be able to

find beauty when they're out

with their friends, out with

people.

Then they will be truly happy.

^ - Charlie

A night sky without stars is as incomplete as a man without a soul.

Not everything is black and white,

there is a lot of gray.

But with some things, you can't deny,

The answer is clear as day.

One's own mind is a fun thing to manipulate.

Twilight happens but once a day.

"I'm not equipped for this existence."
—Chad

"You smell like ... happy" —Tom

Tomorrow is another day

No more 'what-ifs'

If you find yourself saying "I'm not good enough", then tell yourself, "I'll just have to be better."

When you begin to lose grip of your sanity, cling to the things that bring you joy- writing, good friends, or the butterflies.

Smile at the Sparrows

"It seems you too see a painful blue when you stare into the sky" —Conor Oberst

The end is just the beginning of something new.

The trick is to wake up before you get tired.

Don't take breathing for granted.

Take off your iPod and listen to the sounds around you, you won't have them when you're old.

A pleasant suprise will happen when you need it most.

Just because you open your eyes for one night, doesn't mean that you won't close them again in the future.

Change is good.
Sameness is good.
Difference is good.
Apathy is good.

When you stop caring, you stop living.

If you have a story to tell, then you have a life.

It is often bittersweet what new perspective brings

Happiness is like the shriveled little raisin at the bottom of the grape jar.

Try to remember to take a step back every once and a while and remind yourself what you're living for.

"You were distracting me with your wedgy star." -Brooke

"No reason romance" -Chad

Don't be a mental masochist.

Grow in the field, not on the wall.

"It's still yesterday" -Tom

One cannot be inspirational when they are doing what everyone else is doing.

"If the world could remain within a frame like a painting on a wall, I think we'd see the beauty then and stand staring in awe." -Conor Oberst

Remember that one act of kindness can go a surprisingly long way.

Yuppie

Un-coy yourself

I'm only happy most of the time because I go through periods of sadness

So..... milk.

"And what is life? Is it living? Or is it learning to live?" - Matt Rose

Don't undersell your agency.

"It's less than a straw. It's something new entirely" - Chad

The people that give you hope for humanity make the future seem brighter. (Matt Burd)

Find your spot.

"In order to take you have to give what you get"

"The world is only getting smaller and it would only benefit us if we took the time to learn about someone else." - Sundra

Don't get comfortable, reach for the tops of the trees

"I like to feel my feelings" -Matt Burd

There's a blimp crashing outside my window into the clouds.

Don't leave your thoughts incomplete.

The most glorious place in the world is the place that you want to be.

I've been given this. And I've been given that, And it just makes this world so full of trash, I forget.
—Elliot

The Hug - a physical affirmation of reality; and that reality is love.
—Matt

You dance on the pillows that are the clouds of the stars.

It's just life.

You can't seem to soak it in enough, the beauty of the wild, until you realize that you don't have it at home.

The most beautiful world is the one you find inside your own mind.

"You eat that pizza!!" - Tifnay

Once the eery silence of the streets
completes its reverberation, I think
my life, the conceptual indifference
I hide behind my corneas, will
begin to settle back down to normalcy

"Where we're standing right now,
in the ruins in the dark, what
we build could be anything."
~ Chuck

"I don't know what it looks like, but
somewhere inside of me, neurons are
firing accordingly." ~ Danny

"I want to spend the rest of my life
trying to master compassion." - Danny

"Wishing to be happy is not enough"
~ Mr. Mueller

"If you were born into the world as a
human, no matter who you are, there
is one thing you wish above all else:
to be happy." ~ Mr. Mueller

"That may be yours and this may be
mine but I always want to share all
of what is mine with you." ~ Danny

FUCK HATE

"Boredom is the symptom of a rotting mind" ~Mr. Mueller

"You have to make sure you look back on it and say 'I'm glad that happened' instead of 'I wish that could happen again.'" – Tifnay

मत

"You can't get lost. Just turn the page; you are doing the right thing" ~Mr. Mueller

"As one blissful day follows another, your only regret will be for those you lost through your indifference." –Choderlos de Laclos

"No one is indifferent to the quality of their life" ~Mr. Mueller

"What if life was like Hell, do you think we would dream about a life like we have now?" –Alan Ball

"She doesn't know what she's looking for, but she'll know it once she finds it. You won't even choose it, something else will choose it for you." Mr. Mueller

I'm too sheltered to die young
And I'm too jaded to live forever.

Stop wishing and hoping.
Start doing.

Stay where it's fun to live.

We're all alright.

I'm glad life is good. That's how it should be.

The way society sees it, if you're not happy, then it's bad; there is, however, a neutrality that is neither happy or sad and is not necessarily a bad thing. Don't make feeling neutral into a devastating emotion.

Tears do not compromise strength.

Love.

"This must be for real,
cause now I can' feel." -Bush

The world has got me dizzy again.
You'd think after so many years
I'd be use to the spin.

"We can feed this mind of ours in a wise passiveness... our meddling intellect mishapes the beauteous forms of things." -Wordsworth

If you love something give it away.

...Or make it infinite and immortal and just destroy it.

चित

"To lose, I could accept, but to surrender, I just wept." - The Flaming Lips

It's not always your fault.

Accept admiration only after knowing what is admirable.

Think of all the possibilities...

Most perishes with time, one must find something that doesn't

Never regret anything, because at one time, it was exactly what you wanted.

"Everything I love is partly to blame; you are all complicit in the end-result me." - Zach

You can't put the ocean in a bucket.

"Dreams get you through the hard times!" - Running with Scissors

The world is inconceivable as we believe it, but if we try hard enough we will make it reality.

are you at one?

"Losing builds character. Anyone can win, winning is easy."

-Alan Arkin
Little Miss Sunshine

Movies will always help.

"You want to be good at it, you don't want to be bad"

"Darkness within darkness. The gateway to all understanding... create confusion in those who think they know." Lao Tzu

Find the center of your hurricane.

Come what may

-"Why does life so often pull the mat out from under us?" ~Brooke

-"A lot of times, we never even know where we are standing." Zach

You can't script it, not until after it all transpires.

Yes, but, "the tale grows with the telling." J.R.R. Tolkien

All I know is I just don't know.

आनंद

Let it happen.

"When I dipped into the future
far as human eye could see;
I saw the Vision of the world,
and all the wonder that would
be." -Alfred, Lord Tennyson

Blossom as often as possible.

"She was thinking of what might be
brought, not by death, but by life."
-George Eliot

"Just tell me what you feel.
...I'm here for you... my lips
are sealed." -Ken Oak

Hang on.

Today is the first day of the rest
of your life... as is tomorrow...
and the day after.

Write what you know, and if
you don't know it, learn it.

"I hope the exit is joyful &
I hope never to return." -Frida

"Start at ridiculous and work
backwards" -Stranger than Fiction

"At the end of the day we endure
much more than we think
we can." -Frida

"When the darkness passes the light will astound us." -Doc Stoddard

No leaves, just Flowers

It's so easy to make this a Hell...
but with some effort,
a little bit of Heaven shines through.

Don't let yourself be painted by others and Society, or worse be preserved that way. Instead ask for "Sin chete"... be the uncarved block of originality.

Do we really need "something good to die for to make it beautiful to live"?

Sometimes you have to stop.
Just stop. Or you'll go mad.

"We cannot always decipher it precisely in the clear light of our own day." -M. Atwood

Beware the traps of conventionality.

"No lake so still but that it has its wave,
No circle so perfect but that it has its blur.
I would change things for you if I could,
As I can't, you must take them as they are."
-Confucius

"He who feels punctured, must once have been a bubble." -Lao Tzu

SECTION 2:
T.R. in Dark Grey, Brooke in Light Grey

Aside from being rejoiced, loved, and built upon, the List has gone through hardships. It has been mangled, man-handled, ripped, torn, defaced, criticized, slandered, hidden, and stolen. But as in life, through all hardships, the List remains, stronger than ever before. And so here is to a new year with new trials and tribulations, but like the list, we too shall remain strong.

There are bigger things happening here.

All I have is a voice to undo the folded lies. -W.H. Auden

"Something is always going on" -Tom

I'd die for you but I can't live for you.

Know that it's okay to be yourself even if that means being different.

When I close my eyes, the world ends, when I open them in the morning, it begins again.

"Ornament the world with sincerity." -Kerouac

Close your eyes and you'll see more.

"Everything is open. Nothing is supposed to go a certain way." -Tom

"You can have whatever you want, because it's all you." -Brandon

Don't be afraid of going down into the window sill, it will take you to where you most want to be.

"The mystery of God is between two people." -A preacher

"I don't know if anyone can really make a lasting difference, but I certainly want to try." -George Clooney

"Don't distill my mind!! I want racing thoughts!!" -Danny

Its human to want more, that's fine, but while you're on your way to getting it, APPRECIATE what you already have.

Find a place or a way to do good without doing any harm.

The only way to care about yourself is to care about someone else too

"Keep Moving Forward" ~Meet the Robinsons

"You'll always have some excuse not to live your life" ~ Haunted, Chuck Palahniuk

Don't let every pothole you hit be a cause to turn off the road.

Don't let living get in the way of life.

APPRECIATE.

ABOUT THE AUTHOR

While T.R. Dailey is originally from San Diego, she currently resides in Hewitt, New Jersey with her fiancé, two dogs, two cats, and twenty reptiles where she enjoys warm beverages, dystopian novels, and the squirrels chattering about in the trees.

www.ingramcontent.com/pod-product-compliance
Lightning Source LLC
Chambersburg PA
CBHW020551030426
42337CB00013B/1048
9780615963082